Editor
Sara Connolly

Editor in Chief
Ina Massler Levin, M.A.

Creative Director
Karen J. Goldfluss, M.S. Ed.

Illustrator
Clint McKnight

Cover Artist
Marilyn Goldberg

Art Coordinator
Renée Mc Elwee

Imaging
James Edward Grace

Publisher

Mary D. Smith, M.S. Ed.

What's Different?

Grades 5–6

Teacher Created Resources

Author
Christine Smith

Teacher Created Resources
6421 Industry Way
Westminster, CA 92683
www.teachercreated.com

ISBN: 978-1-4206-5908-5

© 2011 Teacher Created Resources
Made in U.S.A.

Teacher Created Resources

Table of Contents

Introduction 3

Science

Water, Water, Everywhere 4

Tornadoes. 5

Man on the Moon 6

Got Coal? 7

Hot Stuff 8

It's in Your Genes 9

Take a Deep Breath 10

Ring of Fire 11

Shake, Rattle, and Roll 12

Don't Get Burned 13

Renewable Resources 14

It's Good to Be on Top 15

Listen to the Waves. 16

Social Studies

Finding the Americas 17

The Real Pocahontas 18

Giving Thanks. 19

Tea Party in Boston 20

The British Are Coming! 21

Let Freedom Ring. 22

Westward Ho 23

Mount Rushmore 24

Clues to the Past 25

Egyptian Hieroglyphs 26

Let the Games Begin 27

The Mystery of the Ark 28

China's First Emperor 29

Circus Maximus 30

Ancient Wonders 31

Math

Happy Birthday! 32

Sweet Geometry. 33

Soccer Puzzler 34

Lucky Ticket 35

Silly Symmetry 36

That's Fast! 37

Math and Technology 38

Record Temperatures 39

How You Slice It 40

Sale! Sale! Sale! 41

Language Arts

Same but Different 42

Where in the World? 43

Knights and Dragons 44

Inspired by History 45

Poetry Without Rhyme 46

Into the Future 47

The Art of Exaggeration 48

Flights of Fantasy 49

Thrill of the Ride 50

Personification 51

Fine Arts

To the Point. 52

On Their Toes 53

Follow the Leader. 54

The Globe Theatre 55

Don't Move 56

An Ear for Music. 57

Answer Key 58

Introduction

The visual puzzles in *Start to Finish: What's Different?* are designed to stimulate thinking skills, support content standards, and entertain students. Each puzzle page presents students with an interesting fact that ties into the classroom curriculum and has two pictures to examine. The students are then challenged to look at the pictures carefully and identify what is different.

Visual puzzles that encourage students to identify differences are more than just fun activities. They reinforce and stimulate critical-thinking and problem-solving skills. As students solve the puzzles, they are improving their observation skills and attention to detail. Their brains are learning to evaluate and analyze visual data through comparison. Students can also work on their fine-motor skills and eye-hand coordination by coloring the pictures.

The puzzles in this book can be used in learning centers, as extension activities, for students who finish early, and as at-home enrichment activities. Have fun learning!

Water, Water, Everywhere

Most of the Earth's surface is covered with water. However, about 97% of it is salt water. That's great if you live in the ocean, but not if you're thirsty.

Look at these pictures. Circle 9 things that are different in the picture above.

Tornadoes

Tornadoes occur around the world, but are most common in an area of the United States known as Tornado Alley. Around 1,000 tornadoes occur in the U.S. annually.

Look at these pictures. Circle 10 things that are different in the picture above.

Man on the Moon

On July 20, 1969, NASA successfully landed the first humans on the moon. Neil Armstrong
was the first astronaut to step out of the lunar module onto the moon.

Look at these pictures. Circle 9 things that are different in the picture above.

Got Coal?

The United States has one of the largest coal reserves in the world. Coal is a fossil fuel that is mined from the ground. It is used to generate about 40% of the world's electricity.

Look at these pictures. Circle 10 things that are different in the picture above.

Hot Stuff

Metals have high melting points and conduct (transfer) heat and electricity from one place to another. That's why pots, pans, irons, and electrical wiring are made of metal.

Look at these pictures. Circle 9 things that are different in the picture above.

It's in Your Genes

Parents pass traits to their children through genes. Your eye color, hair color, blood type, ability to roll your tongue, and much more are determined by your genes.

Look at these pictures. Circle 9 things that are different in the picture above.

Take a Deep Breath

Plants, algae, and cyanobacteria use a process called photosynthesis to make the food they need. This process creates most of the oxygen we breathe.

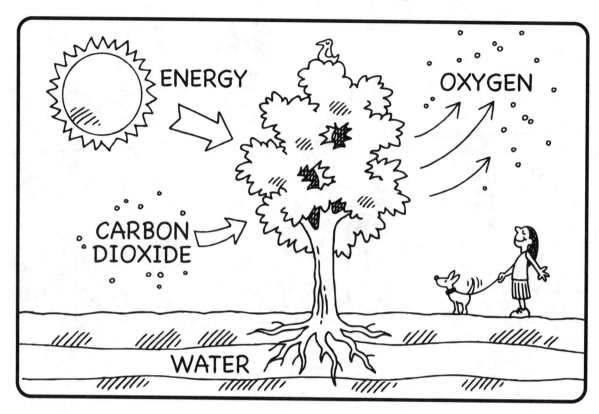

Look at these pictures. Circle 9 things that are different in the picture above.

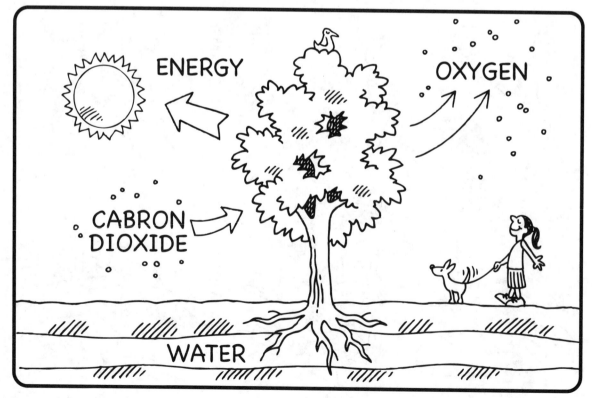

Ring of Fire

Over 75% of the Earth's volcanoes are located along the Pacific Ring of Fire. Several tectonic plates meet along the ring, causing earthquakes and volcanic activity.

Look at these pictures. Circle 9 things that are different in the picture above.

Shake, Rattle, and Roll

Earthquakes are measured using the Richter scale. The strongest quake ever recorded
happened on May 22, 1960, in Valdivia, Chile. It was a magnitude 9.5 quake!

Look at these pictures. Circle 9 things that are different in the picture above.

12

Don't Get Burned

UVA and UVB rays from the sun can cause skin and eye damage, including skin cancer. Water, snow, and ice reflect the rays back at you—increasing your exposure.

Look at these pictures. Circle 10 things that are different in the picture above.

Renewable Resources

Natural resources that can be replaced or are unlimited in supply are renewable. Wind, solar energy, timber, and livestock are examples of renewable resources.

Look at these pictures. Circle 10 things that are different in the picture above.

It's Good to Be on Top

Energy is transferred from one living organism to another through food chains. The top predators help control animal populations and are usually not eaten by other animals.

Look at these pictures. Circle 10 things that are different in the picture above.

Listen to the Waves

Sound travels in waves. The intensity or volume of a sound is measured in decibels. Sounds over 85 decibels can cause damage to the human ear and hearing loss.

Look at these pictures. Circle 10 things that are different in the picture above.

Finding the Americas

After his famous voyage in 1492, Columbus sailed to the Americas three more times. He landed in Central and South America, and the Caribbean, but never North America.

Look at these pictures. Circle 10 things that are different in the picture above.

The Real Pocahontas

Pocahontas lived from around 1595 to 1617. She was the daughter of the Algonquian chief. As a child, she helped the Jamestown colonists by bringing them food.

Look at these pictures. Circle 10 things that are different in the picture above.

Giving Thanks

The Pilgrims celebrated their first harvest in 1621 with the Wampanoag Indians who had helped them. President Lincoln made Thanksgiving a national holiday in 1863.

Look at these pictures. Circle 10 things that are different in the picture above.

19   #5908 Start to Finish: What's Different?

Tea Party in Boston

On December 16, 1773, a group of patriots dressed as Mohawk Indians quietly boarded three ships at Griffin's Wharf. They dumped 342 crates of British tea overboard to protest unfair taxation.

Look at these pictures. Circle 10 things that are different in the picture above.

The British Are Coming!

Paul Revere is famous for his late night ride to Lexington and his role in the American Revolution, but he was also a foundry owner who was known for making church bells.

Look at these pictures. Circle 9 things that are different in the picture above.

Let Freedom Ring

The Liberty Bell was created in 1752 to honor William Penn, Pennsylvania's founder. Since then, the 2,080 lb. bell has become a symbol of freedom in the United States.

Look at these pictures. Circle 10 things that are different in the picture above.

Westward Ho

Many pioneers headed west in the mid-1800s in pursuit of land, gold, and religious freedom.
It took about six months to travel the Oregon Trail (2,000 miles) by wagon.

Look at these pictures. Circle 10 things that are different in the picture above.

23   #5908 *Start to Finish: What's Different?*

Mount Rushmore

Mount Rushmore is located in the Black Hills of South Dakota. It took 14 years and 400 workers to carve the presidential monument using dynamite and jackhammers.

Look at these pictures. Circle 10 things that are different in the picture above.

24

Clues to the Past

Archaeologists study past civilizations. They use clues found at archaeological sites, such as pottery and tools, to learn how people lived before there were written records.

Look at these pictures. Circle 10 things that are different in the picture above.

Egyptian Hieroglyphs

Ancient Egyptians were one of the first civilizations to have a written language. Hieroglyphs were used for formal writing and written on papyrus, wood, or stone.

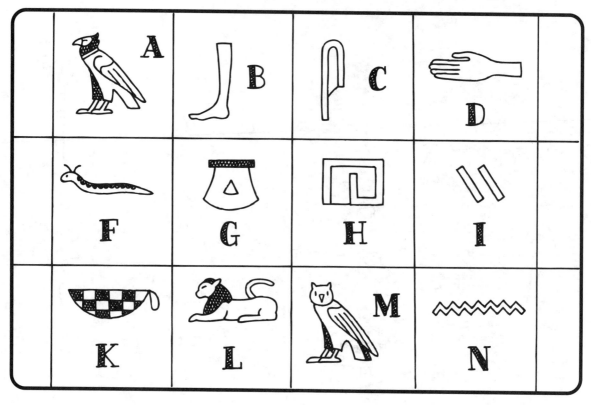

Look at these pictures. Circle 10 things that are different in the picture above.

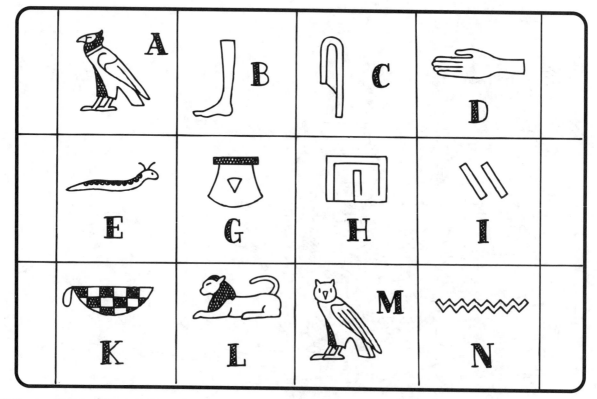

Let the Games Begin

The first Olympic Games took place in Olympia, Greece, in 776 BC. Only freemen who were Greek citizens could compete. The winners received olive branch wreaths.

Look at these pictures. Circle 10 things that are different in the picture above.

The Mystery of the Ark

The greatest treasure of ancient Jerusalem was the Ark of the Covenant. After the Babylonians seized Jerusalem in 586 BC, it went missing. Was it hidden or destroyed?

Look at these pictures. Circle 10 things that are different in the picture above.

China's First Emperor

Qin Shi Huangdi unified ancient China in 221 BC and became its first emperor. He connected and expanded three existing walls to form the first Great Wall of China.

Look at these pictures. Circle 10 things that are different in the picture above.

Circus Maximus

Ancient Romans didn't go to the circus to see clowns. They went to see chariot races.
Circus Maximus was the largest arena at the time and held around 250,000 spectators.

Look at these pictures. Circle 10 things that are different in the picture above.

Ancient Wonders

Of the Seven Wonders of the Ancient World, the Great Pyramid of Giza is the only one that remains. It is the largest pyramid ever built and is made of about 2.3 million stone blocks.

Look at these pictures. Circle 10 things that are different in the picture above.

Happy Birthday!

If today is your birthday, how many minutes until your next birthday? Let's see . . .
365 days x 24 hours a day is 8,760 hours. Then 8,760 hours x 60 minutes
an hour is 525,600 minutes.

Look at these pictures. Circle 10 things that are different in the picture above.

Sweet Geometry

Did you know that bees are good at geometry? Honey bees create honeycomb, clusters of hexagon-shaped cells, out of beeswax to store their honey and young.

Look at these pictures. Circle 10 things that are different in the picture above.

Soccer Puzzler

How much grass is on a soccer field? If the field is 300 feet long and 150 feet wide, we can calculate that there is 45,000 square feet of grass using Area = Length x Width.

Look at these pictures. Circle 10 things that are different in the picture above.

34

Lucky Ticket

Becky bought 5 tickets for the bike raffle. Since 750 tickets were sold, her chances of winning are 5:750 or 1:150. Good luck, Becky!

Look at these pictures. Circle 10 things that are different in the picture above.

Silly Symmetry

A symmetrical shape or object can be divided into two identical halves. Look at the puppets below. The one on the left is symmetrical. The one on the right is not.

Look at these pictures. Circle 10 things that are different in the picture above.

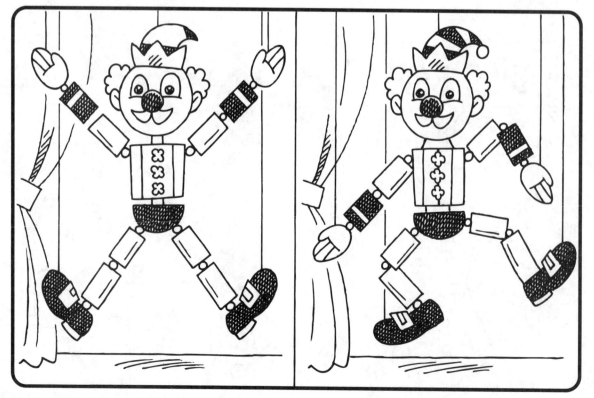

That's Fast!

Cheetahs are the fastest land animal. They can reach speeds of 70 mph! Since there are 60 minutes in an hour, that is 1.17 miles a minute!

Look at these pictures. Circle 10 things that are different in the picture above.

Math and Technology

Storage on computers, smart phones, and MP3 players is measured in bytes. Mega- (1 million), giga- (1 billion), and tera- (1 trillion) are prefixes used to identify the amount.

Look at these pictures. Circle 10 things that are different in the picture above.

Record Temperatures

On the Celsius scale, water freezes at 0 degrees C. Therefore, positive temperatures are above freezing and negative temperatures are below freezing.

Look at these pictures. Circle 10 things that are different in the picture above.

How You Slice It

Chef Pablo loves to cut food into different shapes. He slices oranges (spheres) to make circles and salami (cylinders) to make circles, ovals, and rectangles.

Look at these pictures. Circle 10 things that are different in the picture above.

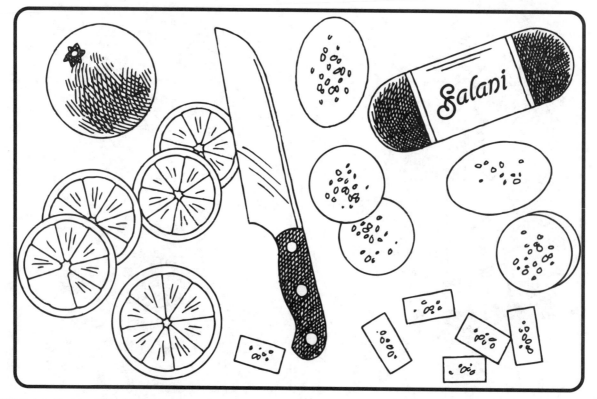

Sale! Sale! Sale!

Pat's Hats is offering 30% off sun hats, 15% off caps, and 20% off cowboy hats. You'll save the most on the cowboy hats because 20% of $34.95 is more than 30% of $19.95.

Look at these pictures. Circle 10 things that are different in the picture above.

Same but Different

Homographs are words that are spelled the same but have different meanings. For example, Tom had to bear twelve pails of food to the bear enclosure this morning.

Look at these pictures. Circle 10 things that are different in the picture above.

Where in the World?

Writers can use real or imaginary settings. *From the Mixed-Up Files of Mrs. Basil E. Frankweiler* is a fictional story set in a real place, the Metropolitan Museum of Art in New York.

Look at these pictures. Circle 10 things that are different in the picture above.

Knights and Dragons

Good versus evil is a common theme in fiction. The conflict creates drama and excitement in the story. That's why brave knights slay evil dragons to save the day.

Look at these pictures. Circle 10 things that are different in the picture above.

Inspired by History

Scott O'Dell often got ideas for his stories by studying the past. *Island of the Blue Dolphins* was inspired by the true story of the lone woman of San Nicolas Island.

Look at these pictures. Circle 10 things that are different in the picture above.

Poetry Without Rhyme

A haiku is a 3-line poem based on syllables, not rhyme. Lines 1 and 3 have 5 syllables.
Line 2 has 7 syllables. This form of poetry originated in Japan and is often about nature.

Run little red crab.

Old man seagull wants his lunch.

Hide, hide in the rocks.

Look at these pictures. Circle 10 things that are different in the picture above.

Run little red crab.

Old men seagull wants his lunch,

Hide. hide in the racks.

Into the Future

Do you want to visit the future or outer space? Then check out science fiction. This genre combines science and imagination to create fascinating stories.

Look at these pictures. Circle 10 things that are different in the picture above.

The Art of Exaggeration

One technique writers use to make their writing more interesting is hyperbole—a form of exaggeration that adds emphasis. For example, "I'm so hungry, I could eat a horse."

Look at these pictures. Circle 10 things that are different in the picture above.

48

Flights of Fantasy

Fantasy stories are characterized by magic and mythical creatures. The Lord of the Rings, The Chronicles of Narnia, and Harry Potter series are examples of this genre.

Look at these pictures. Circle 10 things that are different in the picture above.

Thrill of the Ride

Many stories are like roller coasters. They provide background information and details as they climb toward the climatic event. Then they race down to a solution.

Look at these pictures. Circle 10 things that are different in the picture above.

Personification

Personification uses human characteristics to describe nonhuman things. For example, "Nana's dusty attic was filled with forgotten treasures longing to share their tales."

Look at these pictures. Circle 10 things that are different in the picture above.

To the Point

Pointillism is a technique of drawing or painting that uses dots. Instead of using long strokes of the pen or brush, the artist uses small dots to form the images.

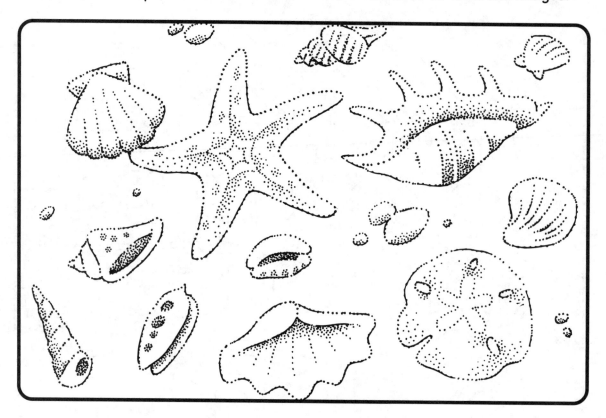

Look at these pictures. Circle 10 things that are different in the picture above.

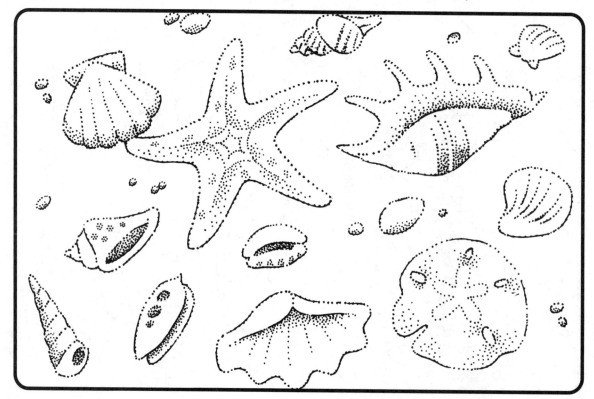

On Their Toes

Ballet requires a lot of physical stamina. Professional ballerinas practice for hours every day. In fact, they practice so much that they wear out several pairs of pointe shoes a week.

Look at these pictures. Circle 10 things that are different in the picture above.

Follow the Leader

A conductor leads orchestra musicians with a baton and gestures. His movements set the tempo (speed) of the music and cue musicians when to come in.

Look at these pictures. Circle 10 things that are different in the picture above.

The Globe Theatre

Shakespeare presented many of his plays in the Globe Theatre. It was built in London in 1598. Later, it was destroyed by fire during a performance and rebuilt in 1614.

Look at these pictures. Circle 10 things that are different in the picture above.

Don't Move

A portrait is a work of art that focuses on the face. It can be a painting, drawing, sculpture, or photograph. The artist may have a person sit for the portrait or work from a photo.

Look at these pictures. Circle 10 things that are different in the picture above.

An Ear for Music

Ludwig van Beethoven (1770–1827) was a classical composer and pianist. Sadly, he lost his hearing and was not able to perform. But that did not stop him from composing.

Look at these pictures. Circle 10 things that are different in the picture above.

Answer Key

Page 4

Page 5

Page 6

Page 7

Page 8

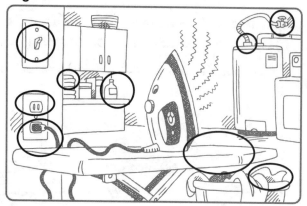

Page 9

Page 10

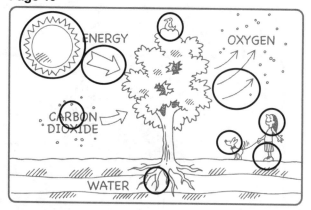

Page 11

Answer Key *(cont.)*

Page 12

Page 16

Page 13

Page 17

Page 14

Page 18

Page 15

Page 19

#5908 Start to Finish: What's Different?

Answer Key (cont.)

Page 20

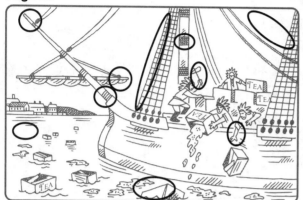

Page 24

Page 21

Page 25

Page 22

Page 26

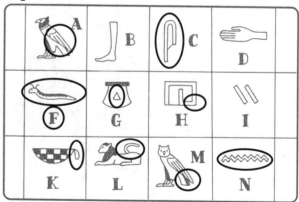

Page 23

Page 27

Answer Key *(cont.)*

Page 28

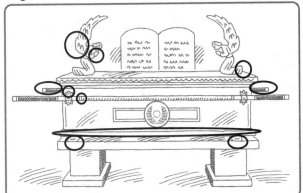

Page 32

Page 29

Page 33

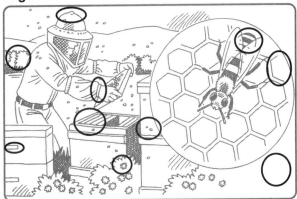

Page 30

Page 34

Page 31

Page 35

Answer Key *(cont.)*

Page 36

Page 37

Page 38

Page 39

Page 40

Page 41

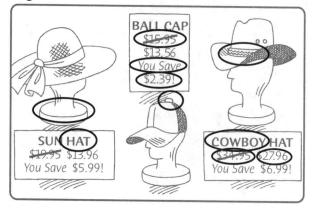

Page 42

Page 43

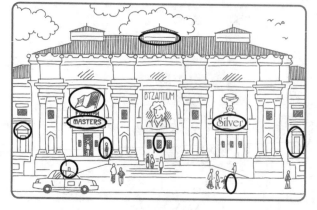

Answer Key *(cont.)*

Page 44

Page 45

Page 46

Run little red crab.

Old man seagull wants his lunch.

Hide, hide in the rocks.

Page 47

Page 48

KITCHEN

Page 49

Page 50

RIDE THE ROCKET

Page 51

Answer Key (cont.)

Page 52

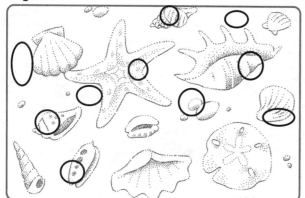

Page 53

Page 54

Page 55

Page 56

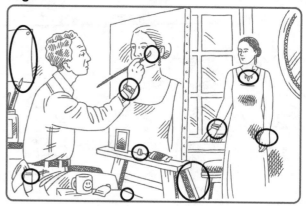

Page 57